Europe: The Crunch

Europe: The Crunch

William Cash, MP

Duckworth

Second impression 1992
First published in 1992 by
Gerald Duckworth & Co. Ltd.
The Old Piano Factory
48 Hoxton Square, London N1 6PB
Tel: 071 729 5986
Fax: 071 729 0015

A catalogue record for this book is available
from the British Library

ISBN 0 7156 2450 4

Acknowledgments

I take this opportunity to thank John Laughland for his continued
assistance, and Colin Haycraft and Deborah Blake of my publishers,
Duckworth, for their encouragement and help. I shall donate half the
royalties from this book to the Red Cross for their work in Bosnia.

Typeset by Ray Davies
Printed in Great Britain by
WBC Print Ltd, Bridgend

Contents

Preface

The past eighteen months have witnessed a profound shift in British policy on Europe. This has coincided with the search for a new alignment in Europe itself in the wake of the reunification of Germany and increasing signs of her assertiveness, the collapse of the USSR and the emergence of the new democracies of Eastern Europe.

Concluding my book *Against a Federal Europe*, published in December 1991 immediately before the signing of the Maastricht treaty, I wrote: 'There is great momentum towards a federal system or something which so closely approximates to one as to be indistinguishable. It is like a Hall of Mirrors. It will take an act of great political will to turn this drift round.'

The one overriding conclusion to be drawn from the Maastricht treaty is that this has not been done. Far from it. The treaty has consolidated the gravitational pull towards federalism, with grave implications for our own and European democracy. This can only be removed by Parliament's refusal to ratify the treaty or, as a last resort, by putting the matter to a referendum, as in the case of Denmark, France and Ireland. Thus at the very least, in the absence of a free vote in Parliament, the individual voters should have an opportunity, as is their right, to have their say on what is by any standards the greatest change in our government for centuries. Maastricht is a turning point in European and British history.

This shift in British policy has been made without so much as a White Paper explaining in straightforward language what is at stake. Even in 1970, when we were deciding whether to join the European Economic Community, there was a White Paper and a free vote in Parliament. In 1975 there was a referendum. Yet in 1991-92 when the issues go to the very heart of our democracy and system of government,

7

all of these are denied to the British people. Attempts have been made to prevent me and others with similar views from being heard, and a national newspaper has even agreed to cease its criticisms of government policy on Europe over the next critical months for the electorate.

All this raises profound and worrying questions – because even the White Paper in 1970 misled them. It promised that there would be 'no question of any erosion of national sovereignty', that the veto would be retained where any one member state considered its vital national interests to be at stake (because otherwise an attempt to impose a minority view 'would imperil the very fabric of the Community') and that 'the Community is no federation of provinces or countries'.

The very fact that these promises were in the 1970 White Paper requires the truth about our loss of veto over monetary union to be spelled out now, even if, for reasons which would be hotly disputed, there are those who would say that we have to move on and that new circumstances require us to acquiesce in a federal arrangement. But worse than this is the fact that it is denied that Maastricht is a federal arrangement. For those who have read the treaty it is all there in black and white. Confused, complex and camouflaged much of it may be, but the reality is clear. We are being taken into a federal system. Federalism, as my previous book showed, has a distinctly poor record. Even single-language Australia is under intense stress.

So why then has Maastricht been signed? This takes us into even more fundamental and difficult political terrain: terrain which threatens the soul of Britain. Maastricht is an exercise in political and economic defeatism. Its supporters, while claiming that it increases our influence, in practice concede that we have lost the political will to stand with confidence within Europe. We have done so for centuries on our own terms but in co-operation with other countries – not tagging along behind Germany in particular and then dressing up concessions to her and to the Eurocrats as victories or as negotiations.

The examples of our loss of confidence and influence are already clear, even before the ink is dry on the treaty. The list of specific instances grows ever longer – our failure over interest rates, our failure to stand firm over the minimum rate of VAT in deference to Chancellor

Kohl's pre-unification tax promises to his own people, the EFA saga, the Franco-German Corps, policy on Yugoslavia, the reappointment of Jacques Delors, etc. Time and again we lose out. We are witnessing a saga of concessions dressed up as negotiations.

And even these specific examples pale into insignificance by comparison with our agreement, in a protocol to the treaty itself, never to veto EMU for Europe as a whole. This concedes the principle and pulls us along in its wake, whatever freedom of manoeuvre our opt-out claims to achieve. It simply defers the question to a later date, by which time it will be too late. The argument that by then it will all have collapsed because it cannot work is too clever and too dangerous by half. Once the treaty is ratified and within the legal framework it prescribes, and under the jurisdiction of the Court of Justice, the tensions felt by the ordinary people of the poorer countries with the betrayal of their expectations will create massive instability and unrest, foreshadowed even now by the repudiation of the Delors II financial package, which itself was based on the new competences signed away at Maastricht. This is the way to ruin trust between the peoples of Europe, not to create it. Similar problems of confusion, uncertainty and tension will flow from the foreign policy provisions of the treaty – legalistic paper provisions which gravely undermine one of our greatest contributions to European affairs over the centuries – our genius for pragmatic decision-taking according to the circumstances of the time.

The underlying defeatism and loss of confidence which Maastricht represents, the strategic failures already revealed since it was signed and the acquiescent, compliant attitudes evidenced by the increasingly one-sided Anglo-German rapprochement of March 1991 show that Maastricht cannot and will not work. The Danish voters have shown, on the unanimity test of the Treaty of Rome itself, that Maastricht has failed for Europe as a whole. Now we can turn the arguments round against federalism as, honour bound, we have always claimed we want to do. Why have we not seized the opportunity? Worse still, why have we even refused to do so?

Meanwhile, German industrialists and bankers have taken up 85 per cent of the foreign investment in Eastern Europe and are driving into the Ukraine. The German Bundesbank relentlessly holds up interest rates all over Europe and the German Government calls upon Europe to pay more towards the reconstruction of Eastern Germany, for which they could provide more but for their industrial expansionism beyond their eastern borders. These are the political dividends of Maastricht, which will be made worse by the European industrial policy, marginalising us even more.

Indeed, as our own recession is fuelled by high German rates to pay for all this within the ERM (now a voluntary commitment but made a legal obligation under Maastricht), and as these bite deeper into our economy with ever-rising unemployment, manufacturing decline, bankruptcies and home repossessions, so our own companies and assets become easy and cheap prey to foreign purchasers, further undermining confidence in a downward spiral. All for what? We do not need the ERM to contain inflation.

Maastricht is a price too high. It is hurting but not working. It stems from a failure of political will when political will has never been more needed. We will not influence Europe from within by emasculating the democratic strength and values upon which our political will has rested for generations. The British people can and will, if given a positive lead and encouragement to turn our economy round, do just that. Maastricht and the ERM merely sap their self-confidence and undermine their pride and initiative.

If Maastricht is not rejected now and if a new treaty is not put in its place at the meeting in Edinburgh in December 1992 under our own Presidency, European, even Western, democracy and stability will be fatally undermined. And this just as the Pacific has become aware of the prospect of a borderless economy and government dominated by Japan. Protectionism and trade wars are written on the global wall while the Third World starves.

We have seen this before. The European crunch is now.

Upton Cressett, August 1992   William Cash

1

Clinging to the wreckage

We are told that Britain is at the heart of Europe, playing her full part in constructing the Community's future. Now is a golden opportunity to do so, for Britain holds the Presidency just when the Franco-German push for federalism, embodied in the Maastricht treaty, has been rejected by the Danish referendum. But instead, the British government is presenting itself as the champion of this breathtaking transfer of powers to the Community. The treaty represented a decisive step towards political integration, but the government is trying to pick up the pieces of other member states' failed plans, rather than taking a lead itself.

Maastricht was wrecked by the Danish vote. The treaty had to be ratified by all twelve member states to enter into force. However uncomfortable this may be for the federalists, Community law now prevents the treaty from going ahead. Coercive suggestions that Denmark should now be excluded from the Community are not only against the spirit of the Community, but also illegal under the Treaty of Rome. It is also utterly anti-democratic to disregard the Danish vote in this way.

Edinburgh, where the summit at the end of our Presidency is to take place in 1992, should be the site of a new, renegotiated treaty. Now that the Franco-German project has fallen apart, Britain has a duty, as President, to work in favour of Europe as a whole, insisting that it turn away from the federalism and anti-democratic bureaucracy of Maastricht, and towards a union of democratic nation-states in Europe, which are the only basis for proper democracy.

2

Always keep a hold of nurse, for fear of finding something worse

We are told that there should be no renegotiation of Maastricht, and that there would be an institutional paralysis if the Maastricht deal became unravelled.

The government have admitted that they are afraid of unpicking the treaty, in case new pressures for greater centralisation return. This does not say much for confidence in their capacity to influence Europe's development. However, in the government's initial reaction to the result, it was suggested that a new clause should be added to the treaty in order to pacify Danish worries about sovereignty. It has been argued that this might be achieved by adding new administrative procedures to Article 3b (the 'subsidiarity' clause). But how can this occur without amending and thereby renegotiating the treaty?

Maastricht cannot be ratified in its present form. It has already become unravelled. Suggestions that there should be a second referendum in Denmark will only entrench the dangerous drift in the Community away from democratic accountability, and further undermine the principle of a national veto on new developments in the Community. If the intention is to allow Denmark to opt out of Maastricht while remaining in the Community (logistically an almost impossible task) then the new treaty will have to be renegotiated. The argument that we must forge on regardless of the Danish vote shows a worrying contempt not only for clearly expressed democratic choice, but also for reality.

Edinburgh should take the first step back to reality. If Maastricht is not ratified, the Treaty of Rome and the Single European Act still remain. There will be no institutional crisis. In 1954, the French

National Assembly rejected the European Defence Community, to general shock and amazement. But within three years, the much better Treaty of Rome had been negotiated and signed. Douglas Hurd has agreed that the Maastricht negotiations took place too soon for British liking after the Single European Act. Other peoples in Europe, particularly in France and Germany, have belatedly woken up to the implications of the treaty negotiated in their names by their governments. Without a new treaty, taking Europe down a more democratic and balanced route than Maastricht, we will be shirking our responsibilities to the Community and to Europe as a whole.

3

Little Englanders or Great Europeans?

We are told that the choice is between accepting Maastricht or repudiating the European Community as a whole. To be anti-Maastricht is said to be anti-European. This is an insular argument, which assumes that the only question for the British is whether they should be in or out. But nobody wants to see Britain standing alone outside Europe. The questions it raises are much broader. Any argument based on this unreal alternative is untenable and anti-Community.

Maastricht is a treaty for exclusion, not inclusion. It destroys the notion of a Europe of Twelve, and replaces it with a Europe of concentric circles, based around an inner core. It will exclude the poorer countries of the EC from influence. It is already threatening to exclude Denmark. It threatens to exclude Eastern Europe, both economically and politically.

At the Maastricht summit, the British government could have insisted that the Community must move ahead as twelve. Instead of this, it was itself party to a proposal that monetary union should be constructed by stages, with less than twelve countries to begin with. This was a crucial concession to the German desire to create a Europe of concentric circles, with Germany geographically and politically at the centre. It is bad for the Community, and it is bad for Europe as a whole, especially the East, which is already falling prey to excessive German domination. It represents a great failure of political will that Britain decided that it had to accept EMU for fear of being left out by the others.

Edinburgh lies at the periphery of a country which is itself geographically on the edge of Europe. Anybody who looks at a map can see that Britain is not at the heart of Europe. This is our advantage. To be sure, we must be heartily involved in the Community, and in the wider

Europe. But our foreign policy should exploit our incontrovertible geopolitical situation, which gives us a wider perspective, and a certain healthy scepticism. As Churchill said, 'We are with Europe, but not of it. We are linked, but not comprised. We are interested and associated, but not absorbed' (11 May 1953). He added: 'We do not intend to be merged in a European federal system.' Our history and our involvement in Europe in war and peace for centuries – our role in the last two World Wars – prove our European credentials, precisely because of our commitment to freedom and democracy now under threat from the Maastricht treaty. This commitment makes us, as it has made us in the past, Great Europeans – not Little Englanders.

EMU should have been rejected by us at Maastricht; now Maastricht has been rejected by the Danes. Given the failure of Maastricht, Britain should be putting herself at the heart of the wider Europe by trying to deflect the Community from its inward-looking and undemocratic integration plans, and championing the causes of the those countries outside the twelve who would lose out from the creation of this concentrated superstate in the middle of the continent. But we should not ourselves commit political suicide by accepting this geopolitical scheme and placing ourselves on the political periphery by so doing. We are not Euro-sceptics, we want a different kind of Europe, not the exclusive and undemocratic Europe represented by Maastricht. Europe has always been at its most creative and enterprising when its nation states have been competitive. Building real democracy into this formula is the truly European way forward within the existing treaty framework.

4

Maastricht: no victory for Britain

We are told that opposing Maastricht would mean sitting on the sidelines of Europe. We are told that we must either accept this Franco-German initiative or sit, carping, outside the charmed inner circle of powerful countries.

Maastricht was concocted by Germany and by the moribund French socialist government attempting to find new ways of containing her resurgent neighbour, after President Mitterrand had failed to prevent reunification itself. Germany needs a figleaf of respectability for her new assertiveness, and has for long wanted to establish a German-centred united Europe, based around a Deutsche Mark zone and a federal union modelled on herself.

Germany, in particular, was delighted at her success at Maastricht. The planned European Central Bank is modelled on the German central bank; federalism is inspired by Germany. All of the key demands of the Germans were fulfilled. The German Finance Minister has written, 'We are introducing our Deutsche Mark into Europe via EMU.' Germany regards France's belief that EMU and federalism will contain her with a certain benign amusement, for the time being.

Britain seemed unable to stand up for its principles, or to argue for a clear alternative.

Much of what Britain did in the negotiations was to water down the worst excesses of the earlier drafts of the treaty, which may have been mere negotiating stances anyway. We abandoned the possibility of vetoing monetary union for the whole of Europe. But the argument that we cannot say 'No' if we wish to preserve our influence is as convincing as would be a backbench MP who always voted with the government, and then claimed that they listened to what he said.

A new **Edinburgh** treaty would show that influence comes from leading, not following. The other big countries in the Community (France, Germany, Italy) are temporarily preoccupied with internal political difficulties; while the British presidency, and the recent general election victory, place us in a new position of influence. Yet if we do not insist on renegotiation of the treaty we are not taking advantage of this new position, either because we apparently want the treaty or for fear of standing apart from the crowd. Other countries use their presidencies to influence Europe as a whole: so should we.

5

Britain's lost influence in Europe: appeasing the federalists

We are told that Britain is already beginning to influence Europe. It is argued that the treaty is the first decentralising measure, and that it represents a defeat for the federalists. Yet during the general election the Conservative Party MEPs officially and formally consummated their integration (initiated by the former Chairman of the Party with the support of the Prime Minister) with the exclusively federalist European People's Party.

Maastricht is a crypto-federalist treaty. The removal of the word 'federal' makes no difference, for, as one German federalist has written, 'The Treaty on European Union establishes federalism and subsidiarity as structural principles, and introduces new elements which can be considered as cornerstones of a European constitution.'

It creates a Union, with a European citizenship. It refers to 'the territory of the Union', its 'coherence', 'solidarity', and 'borders', as if the Union were a country in its own right. It imposes new duties on 'citizens of the Union'. 'The Union' becomes a legally enforceable entity under international and Community law. The United Kingdom is subsumed into 'the Union', and Article F refers to 'its member states'.

As Jacques Delors has urged, subsidiarity is a federalist concept, and its formulation in Maastricht is copied from the German constitution. It was not a British initiative.

Few European governments on the Continent are convinced by the British government's supposedly new European commitment, and many are still intensely suspicious of it. The failure at Lisbon to achieve any progress on enlargement, the fudge on monetary union (not saying yes, not saying no, abandoning the veto), the failure to stem Community spending, the failure to nip the Commission's abuse of its powers in the bud, the capitulation over the Community's right to stipulate tax levels and employment law ... one searches in vain for real evidence of British influence and asks, 'What do we gain from all this?'

Edinburgh should regain a British initiative in Europe by presenting a clearly different Europe, a Europe which does not try to ignore democratic nationhood, as Maastricht does. There is considerable support for such an approach among ordinary people in Britain and in other EC countries, where the European debate has only recently started. What evidence is there that, apart from Denmark, there has been any serious attempt to consult the individual people of Europe about the specific provisions contained in Maastricht?

6

For Europe's sake – No

We are told that Maastricht responds to the needs of a changing Europe.

Maastricht is as wrong for the rest of Europe as it is for Britain. For two years now, since the fall of the Berlin Wall and the subsequent changes in Eastern Europe and the former Soviet Union, the Community has repeatedly failed to respond to the imperative of the moment, which is to rebuild the whole continent through free trade and committed political cooperation. The treaty should have addressed the problems of the whole of Europe, instead of concentrating on the concerns of a few who have grafted the obsolete solutions of the 1950s on to the problems of the 1990s.

At a conference in Paris earlier this year, Bronislaw Geremek, one of the founding fathers of Solidarity, publicly asked Jacques Delors whether the Community was ready to give a clear sign of encouragement to the nascent democracies of the East. Delors promised that such a declaration would come at the Lisbon summit. It was a promise easily given, and easily forgotten, for at the Lisbon summit there was no decisive declaration on Eastern Europe, just a row about the budgetary contribution instead. Maastricht is a missed opportunity, taking Europe in the opposite direction from that in which she ought to be going, compounded by the massive problems presented by the removal of borders which are in prospect.

For Europe's sake, **Edinburgh** should provide the breadth and depth of true political leadership, and a proper, mature understanding of our political obligations and moral duties to the East, not the narrow vision of the bureaucrat, nor the unimaginative policy of a 'safe pair of hands'. The border provisions must be re-examined and renegotiated, whichever treaty they come from.

7

The eclipse of democracy

We are told that Maastricht reinforces accountability in the European Community, bringing power closer to the citizen.

Maastricht is striking for its deeply anti-democratic character. It was drawn up in secret, without a White Paper, and will not be the subject of a free vote in the House of Commons, nor of a referendum. It vests the central powers of government in the hands of unaccountable bankers and commissioners, shielding them from any democratic accountability and taking them as far away from the voters as it is possible to get. So much for 'subsidiarity'.

It was drawn up with a mistrust of voters. After the Danish vote, Wilfred Maartens, MEP, said that he thought referenda were dangerous because they sometimes produced unexpected results. One German commentator has written, 'More and more frequently elections are now distorting themselves into an instrument of protest for the voters ... Unless Europe soon encounters a new type of voter, governing will become even more difficult than it was in the past' (*German Comments*, July 1992). Quite what 'a new type of voter' is, he does not say. Indeed, after the Danish vote, a Swedish paper commented that, in its opinion, Maastricht was supported by the governments of Europe because they were fed up with having to be accountable to their own parliaments, and preferred to decide policy among themselves behind closed doors. Such a fear of freedom and withdrawal of political responsibility laid the foundations of Fascism in the 1930s.

Edinburgh should try to turn around this anti-democratic drift. Britain should emphasise her traditional strengths of open, parliamentary government, and try to ensure that it takes root all over Europe. We should start by insisting that the other countries of the EC adopt measures for the scrutiny of legislation and the accountability of national governments to their parliaments of the kind with which we are familiar in Britain and Denmark. Democracy is even more important than price stability. With a full democracy we can choose our own price stability. Without freedom of choice and democracy we cannot choose at all.

8

Decision-making structures

We are told that decision-making structures have been improved.

Maastricht has failed to address the most glaring defects of the Community. The Commission is in the unique position of being an unelected bureaucracy which has the exclusive right of initiative over all EC legislation. This is an anachronistic and anti-democratic state of affairs. Maastricht notably failed to reduce the Commission's power, or to nip its tendency to abuse its powers in the bud: on the contrary, it increased its power and created confusion and uncertainty with the introduction of 'subsidiarity'.

The legislative procedures of the EC leave too little room for accountability. Where votes are taken by unanimity, each individual minister in the Council is accountable to his national parliament, at least in theory, for not having vetoed a particular bill. Some majority voting may be tolerable in the Single European Act, which was concerned with establishing free trade throughout the Community, but Maastricht exacerbates this procedure by extending it to areas of government itself.

At **Edinburgh,** Britain should argue that the Community has come of age, and no longer needs the tight centralist dirigisme of the 1950s to hold it together. On the contrary, in a wider Europe, a tight central core will introduce impossible tensions, especially where financial transfers of resources to the poorer countries fail to materialise. The Commission's role should be reduced to that of a secretariat, returning the full right of political initiative to the Council of Ministers, accountable to national parliaments. The individual members of the Council should be given a clear right of veto, as an essential safeguard.

9

National parliaments and the nation-state

We are told that the role of national parliaments has been strengthened, and that federalism has been rejected. We were told that the European Parliament would not be able to overrule the Council by means of a 'co-decision' procedure.

Maastricht contains nothing but a simple 'declaration' encouraging the national parliaments to take a greater interest in Community affairs. This is because very few of them currently scrutinise European legislation. For over thirty years, France has been a member of the EC without ever submitting European bills to the National Assembly beforehand. The 'declaration' in the treaty is of doubtful importance: it is placed next to a similar declaration on the protection of animals. If Maastricht is ratified, national parliaments will, indeed, be threatened with extinction unless they do something about it now.

Maastricht introduces a 'co-decision' procedure, which enables the European Parliament to overrule a decision taken by the Council of Ministers, in a whole new range of areas (Article 189 b (2c)). Thus, individual countries can be outvoted not only by other countries in the Council, but also by the European Parliament. The usual federalist reply to this is that the role of the European Parliament should be strengthened.

Edinburgh should refute this argument. The co-decision procedure is a cause for concern, because it represents another click of the ratchet towards establishing the European Parliament as a federal parliament. The new provisions for accountability of the Commission to the Parliament also point clearly in a federalist direction, for they suggest that the Commission is a European government in embryo.

Those who think that the European Parliament can ever adequately replace the true accountability and openness which is characteristic of the Westminster parliament are showing their own ignorance of what a parliament really is. The European Parliament will become increasingly ineffective as it grows larger, with its myriad languages, greatly increased numbers and increasing remoteness from voters. Parliamentary democracy is a complex and delicate thing, robust when exercised, but which can wither and die if its inherent values are neglected, or if it falls into disuse or disrepute. If we want to preserve democracy we must insist that Europe as a whole does not hand the central powers of government to unelected bankers and the unaccountable Commission.

Our open and accountable parliamentary system in Britain is a great historical inheritance, and many European countries, including several in the Community, would rightly be jealous of it. A glance at the political culture of France or Italy shows how difficult it is to achieve a mature parliamentary democracy. It is not something which can be created out of the blue by a legislative act, but is the achievement of generations.

10

Monetary union: the illusion of the British opt-out

We are told that Britain successfully rejected federalism, but monetary union, which Britain has not rejected, is the very centrepiece of Maastricht's covert federalism. We are told that the 'opt-out' from monetary union keeps our options open.

Maastricht commits its signatories to 'the establishment of an economic and monetary union, including ... a single currency', and it declares that, under Stage 2 of EMU, to which Britain is committed by Maastricht, 'the European Monetary Institute shall prepare the instruments and procedures for carrying out a single monetary policy in the third stage'.

While he was Chancellor, the Prime Minister declared, 'Although entry to the Exchange Rate Mechanism is part of our commitment to Stage 1 of economic and monetary union and the single market, it in no sense commits us to the Delors approach for stages 2 or 3. I assure the House that there has been no shift, no weakening in our opposition to the imposition of a single currency and a single monetary authority. We remain opposed to that' (23 October 1990).

Maastricht legally commits us to the practical implications of having the whole of the Treasury, the Bank of England and the civil service machinery setting up the European Monetary Institute. It is incredible to imagine that the gravitational pull of this would allow us to stand aside at the last minute.

The final decisions on economic convergence are to be taken by majority voting before 31 December 1996, within the lifetime of this parliament. Thus, by agreeing to Maastricht now, we are agreeing that Britain will submit herself to a majority vote of other countries on her future. By signing the treaty, we are locking ourselves into this process.

Moreover, there is no indication that Britain intends to stand outside a future monetary union. As Tristan Garel-Jones, Minister of State at the Foreign Office, emphasised on 27 February 1992 in reply to the author, 'We do not reject a single currency, nor do we reject any of the institutions that go with it.'

This stance derives from the apparent belief that whatever happens, Britain cannot stop monetary union from going ahead. Far from being a gain, the opt-out is the worst of all worlds. By agreeing to it, and by accepting the concentric circles approach implicit in the convergence criteria and the staggered approach to EMU, we have enshrined this admission of defeat in law, ensuring that such a veto is legally impossible. EMU is undesirable for the whole continent, and is the centrepiece of the federalist project. By giving in on this, the government, which claims to have won some important battles at the Maastricht summit, has in fact lost the whole war. Instead of negotiating at the heart of Europe, with the interests of the whole continent in mind, the British government has been arguing on the sidelines while accusing those against Maastricht of doing so themselves.

Edinburgh should make up for these omissions. Opposition to EMU is based on the democratic principle that the control of the monetary, economic and fiscal policies of the European Community cannot and should not be concentrated in the hands of unaccountable bankers, and that the future development of the Community cannot go against the grain of existing nations and their political institutions. These principles have been enunciated by the Prime Minister, the Chancellor, the Foreign Secretary, and even the Leader of the Opposition. None the less, we seem to have caved in. The decision against monetary union must be taken now at Edinburgh.

The 'irrevocable process': a conveyor belt to federalism

We are told that the decision on EMU remains for the British parliament to take when the time is right. Our own opt-out was claimed to represent our objections to the present proposals for the Central Bank and a single currency. Following the Danish referendum it would be consistent with our opt-out to repudiate these now.

Maastricht contains a protocol, adjacent to the British 'opt-out', which, far from safeguarding British and European interests, stipulates that:

> The High Contracting Parties declare the irreversible character of the Community's movement to the third stage of Economic and Monetary Union by signing the new Treaty provisions on Economic and Monetary Union.
>
> Therefore, all Member States, whether they fulfil the necessary conditions for the adoption of a single currency or not, shall respect the will for the Community to enter swiftly into the third stage, and therefore no Member State shall prevent the entering into the third stage.
>
> If by the end of 1997 the date of the beginning of the third stage has not been set, the Member States concerned, the Community institutions and other bodies involved shall expedite all preparatory work during 1998, in order to enable the Community to enter the third stage irrevocably on 1 January 1999 and to enable the ECB and the ECSB to start their full functioning from this date.
>
> This protocol shall be annexed to the Treaty establishing the European Community.

Thus, by signing the treaty now, Britain rules out a veto on this process (which is part of the Treaty of Rome and within the competence of the European Court of Justice) and puts her signature to its 'irreversibility'.

Edinburgh should reverse Maastricht. Britain needs to insist on preserving a balance of democratic power and interest across the Community. To accept the irreversible process towards a monetary union for a tight core of powerful countries at the centre of the continent, grouped around Germany, would be to deny the future of the Community of twelve, and to accept the creation of a continental superstate, whether Britain was in it or not.

The illusion of an independent central bank

We are told that Economic and Monetary Union will contribute to price stability in the European Community because the bank will be independent of political control by governments. It is here that the federalists' arguments are at their most explicitly anti-democratic: they believe that one must reduce the degree of control of democratically elected and accountable politicians as far as possible.

Maastricht proposes a Central Bank which will not be independent of political control, it will merely be independent of democratic control. It will be controlled by majority voting in the Council, and dominated by Germany, where trade balances hold the key to European commerce. As the President of the Bundesbank has repeatedly made clear, it is impossible to separate monetary policy from the rest of government policy. He has said, 'The entire environment must be geared to the stability of the monetary system, meaning both financial policy, and, moreover, social policy.'

The Bundesbank, which has served as the model for the Central Bank, is under the effective control of the German government. It is false to say that it is independent: Article 12 of the Bundesbank's constitution obliges it to support the economic policies of the government. When the Germans decided to raise interest rates in July 1992, readers of the *Financial Times* will have noticed a front-page photograph of the Economics Minister, Jurgen Mollemann, arriving in a Luftwaffe helicopter to attend the meeting at which the decision was made. It is wrong to imagine that the Bundesbank does not want EMU. It has described monetary union as 'an irrevocable sworn confraternity' requiring political union. In May 1992 its President described EMU as 'a veritable leap forward'.

In the same way, the European Central Bank will not be any more independent of political control than other central banks, such as the Federal Reserve in the United States. Nicholas Brady, Secretary of the Treasury, in August 1992 said he would support legislation to enhance the role of Congress in the decision-making of the Fed. But Congress is directly elected. Norman Lamont has confirmed that the Council of Ministers will exercise control over the Bank's governing council. But who will control them? And which country will exercise most influence? There are no prizes for guessing – Germany. The only respect in which it will be independent is that it will, unfortunately, be outside any democratic control. Our budgets will be 'capped', further reducing our voters' choices over health, education, social security, local government and other areas – even defence.

The treaty is explicit on this matter: with respect to Europe as a whole, it says that the European System of Central Banks will be obliged to 'support the general economic policies of the Community with a view to contributing to the achievement of the objectives of the Community as laid down in Article 2'. Article 2 says:

The Community shall have as its task, by establishing a common market and an economic and monetary union and by implementing the common policies or activities referred to in Articles 3 and 3A, to promote throughout the Community a harmonious and balanced development of economic activities, sustainable and non-inflationary growth respecting the environment, a high degree of convergence of economic performance, a high level of employment and of social protection, the raising of the standard of living and quality of life, and economic and social cohesion and solidarity among Member States.

Article 3, in its turn, defines the activities of the Community as: elimination of trade barriers, common commercial policy, the internal market, free movement of persons, agriculture and fishing, transport policy, competition policy, approximation of national law for the common market, social policy, economic and social cohesion, envi-

31

ronmental policy, industrial policy, trans-European networks, health policy, education and culture, development policy, association with overseas territories, consumer protection, energy, civil protection and tourism. The bank will be legally obliged to support the overall policy of the Community in all these areas: so much for independence. All this is in the absence of any proper definition of 'price stability'.

Edinburgh should take note of the recent warnings by the IMF and the Bank of International Settlements against EMU and by anti-inflationary economists such as Milton Friedman, who have attacked EMU as a potential source of inflation: the bank would have all these other priorities to consider, as well as the effect of its decisions on the weaker economies of the Community. It should arrest and turn around the traditional development of the Community along excessively bureaucratic lines. It should promote a system of free currency competition, whether between national or private monetary policies, and it should emphasise that, far from liberalising monetary policy from political control, EMU simply reimposes it at the European level, without the safeguard of democracy.

Subsidiarity: a recipe for centralisation

We are told that the so-called 'principle' of subsidiarity will contribute to decentralisation. On his return from Oslo after the Danish referendum, Douglas Hurd indicated that the way the treaty worked in practice was seen by the Danes and by the House as more important than what is written down. This cannot be so. The European Community is a legal order, which entails clearly defined obligations.

Maastricht contains a clear obligation 'to maintain in full the "acquis communautaire" ' (Article B), i.e. the exisiting powers of the Community. Far from encouraging devolution of power back to the nation-states, this article explicitly rules it out.

Secondly, the 'subsidiarity' test applies to all policy areas not already within the Community's exclusive competence. The Community is empowered to extend its powers if Community action is deemed more 'effective' than national action. Far from being a recipe for decentralisation, therefore, the subsidiarity article can only be used for centralisation. As Jacques Delors has written, 'Subsidiarity ... is an obligation for the higher authority to act vis-à-vis a person or a group in order to see that it is given the means to achieve its ends.' The treaty itself, of course, adds a whole host of new powers to the Community (see Section 12 above), leaving hardly any area of policy untouched.

The formulation of the subsidiarity principle in the Maastricht treaty mirrors a similar clause in the German Constitution, and Germany has witnessed incessant centralisation since the Federal Republic was founded.

It is inconsistent to champion a treaty which transfers the most important powers of government to the Community, while boasting that an unusable, undefinable and question-begging article might be invoked to get them back again. Why transfer them in the first place? Resistance to Community interference in the 'nooks and crannies' of our national life, which we profess to want, needs treaty revisions if we are to strike at the heart of the matter. Merely backing off from unpopular current directives does not solve the real problem, which is excessive treaty powers. Furthermore, if, as the government claims, the Community was becoming excessively intrusive by abusing its powers under the Single European Act, why were not legally binding provisions included in the Maastricht treaty to nip them in the bud?

One constitutional lawyer has concluded, 'The doctrine of "subsidiarity" is, without profound institutional reform or changes of attitude or both, virtually worthless as a protection against further unwanted expansion of the European law and institutions into further aspects of national life. It may, in fact, be worse than worthless if, by giving an illusion of protection, it encourages agreement to measures which would not otherwise be agreed to' (Martin Howe, *Europe and the Constitution after Maastricht*). Subsidiarity has been described by a former President of the Court of Justice as 'gobbledegook' and severely criticised by serried ranks of lawyers expert in European law.

Even if the subsidiarity principle could be used for devolving power (and the way it is formulated prohibits this) the decision on whether to do so would be taken by the European Court of Justice, whose integrationist tendencies are well known. Moreover, rulings of the Court of Justice apply only once acts of Community law have been passed, not before. The damage is done first, and then the vain attempts to rectify it will follow.

The use of 'effectiveness' as a standard does, of course, beg the question. If you want to introduce a Community-wide policy on anything at all, then clearly the institutions of the Community are the most 'effective' means of doing it. The 'effectiveness' standard is undesirable, revealing the managerial-authoritarian philosophy which runs through every line of the treaty. Sooner or later a really objectionable policy will be introduced by the Community under the label 'more effective'. Any opposition to it will be swept aside under the ominous carte blanche given by Article F(3): 'The Union will provide itself with the means necessary to attain its objectives and carry out its policy.'

Far from bringing power closer to the people, Maastricht alienates them from it. It vests decision-making power in unelected and democratically unaccountable bodies, concentrating the most important governmental responsibilities in a granite centre of power, as far from ordinary people as possible, which will become even clearer as cobwebs in the nooks and crannies are swept away. It corresponds to the socialist model of according the 'commanding heights' of the economy to the state. In arrogating to itself the power to legislate in scores of policy areas, the Maastricht treaty will widen the gulf between government and the governed, creating a sullen resentment against distant power, rather than ready, responsible, popular involvement and identification with it. Subsidiarity is part of the problem, not the solution.

Edinburgh should become a signpost away from such thinking and should dismantle by treaty the power of the Commission to initiate legislation as at present. Instead of invoking 'effectiveness' as a standard, it should invoke 'democratic': the question should be, 'How can the Community be run most democratically?' Why did the government not insist on this at the time? The panic withdrawal of individual directives in the name of subsidiarity does not deal with the real problem, which is centralisation and the way the Commission works.

The Luxembourg compromise

We are told that nothing in the treaty will affect the sovereignty of parliament. But an easy way to prevent interference in the national affairs of a country, or to prevent the Community from moving in an undesirable direction, is to make it inoperative under Community law. When Britain joined the Common Market in 1972, it had operated for several years on the principle established by General de Gaulle in 1965, known as the 'Luxembourg Compromise'. This enabled a country to veto Community legislation for the Community as a whole if it thought its essential national interests were jeopardised by proposed new developments. Moreover, de Gaulle rejected supranationalism in general, and most decisions were taken by unanimity.

But **Maastricht** embodies the principle that no individual country has the right to say 'No' on matters of vital national interest. It abolishes any hope that the Luxembourg compromise could ever be invoked. The general reaction to the Danish referendum, supported by the British, which was to plough on regardless, entrenches the principle that one single state cannot use the veto. The British opt-outs on monetary union and social policy underline this. Indeed the very threat, made repeatedly by France and Germany against Britain as monetary union was being discussed, and now made to Denmark (by Valéry Giscard d'Estaing and Chancellor Kohl, among others), that recalcitrant countries could be excluded from the Community if they did not agree with its future plans, show a striking lack of Community spirit, not to mention a contempt for the law and electorates which is far worse. If the Maastricht treaty is rejected by one or more countries, the Treaty of Rome remains. Any attempt to force a member state out would be clearly illegal, and justiciable before the International Court at the Hague.

Edinburgh should incorporate the Luxembourg compromise by formulating it for the first time in the treaty. Its existence as a weapon of last resort would serve as a healthy brake on undue pressure on unwilling countries. We must also show the political will to use it. All member states must be able to agree about the Community's present functioning and future development. It is not sufficient simply to defend oneself against excessive interference: we must take the interests of Europe as a whole into account.

15

The illusion of decentralisation

We are told that Maastricht is a decentralising measure, and that Britain has succeeded in turning around the incessant centralisation of the European Community. It is an ambiguous argument, because it seems to play on the instinctive British dislike of its undemocratic practices, while at the same time arguing that we should be at the heart of it.

Maastricht does not say this. The treaty makes a huge transfer of new powers to the Community, especially in economic, monetary, fiscal and social policy, significantly reinforcing its federal nature. Moreover, it is precisely the most important powers of government which are to fall within the Community's competence, vested in unelected, undemocratic and unaccountable institutions such as the central bank and the Commission.

Quite apart from being simply wrong, this claim that Maastricht decentralises concedes an important principle if presented in these terms, namely that the Community is a 'centre'. The use of the word 'decentralisation' explicitly accepts that sovereignty (ultimate legal authority) resides in the Community, from which individual powers may or may not be devolved.

The government argues that the Maastricht treaty is less centralised than the earlier Dutch and Luxembourg drafts. It may be true that the British conducted some kind of damage-limitation operation, achieving an outcome which was marginally less undesirable than was feared at first, but it is mistaken to say that Maastricht is less centralising than the Single European Act. Moreover Maastricht is above all about government.

An Edinburgh treaty should remove this ambiguity. The Community should not be regarded as a 'centre', for the nation-states should guard their legal and effective sovereignty. This can be done both by refusing to transfer excessive new powers to the Community's institutions, and by making provision for the protection of national interests, where necessary, by national law. Any suggestion that a mere appeal for a more decentralised community would prevent the Commission and the Court from pursuing their customary integrationist policies is simply an exercise in hope over experience.

The illusion of the pillars of Maastricht

We are told that the Maastricht treaty has succeeded in overcoming the excessive centralism of the European Community by placing certain aspects of its new powers under intergovernmental arrangements, known as 'pillars', which do not fall within the institutional structure of the Treaty of Rome. It is argued that this reduces the power of the Commission, and that 'Brussels' would no longer be involved in certain areas.

Maastricht begins with a commitment to 'a single institutional framework'. The great bulk of new policy areas will fall within the competence of the Treaty of Rome. The most important of these is the central bank and monetary union. Moreover, the institutions of the Community are always involved in the formulation of policy, even in the 'pillars'. The Commission is 'fully associated' with the preparation of foreign policy and justice and home affairs (Articles J. 5.3 and K.4.2).

Thus the central institutions of the Community (Commission, Court and Council) will sit sometimes as the 'Union' (in the case of foreign policy, and justice and home affairs, the two 'pillars'), and sometimes as the 'European Community'. Given that the Community itself has a myriad of different modes of operation (there are a dozen decision-taking mechanisms already, and five different ways of involving the parliament, depending on the subject matter under discussion), the difference between a 'pillar' and the 'European Community' proper will be largely invisible to the outside observer. Indeed, it will not be long before they are all harmonised into one structure, since by then people will argue, with some justification, that the difference between the Union and the EC itself is little more than a technicality.

Indeed, the confusion between the 'Union' and the 'Community' already exists. The 'Citizenship of the Union' is established by Articles 8 – 8e of the Treaty of Rome, as amended by Maastricht, and as such it is subject to the adjudication of the Court of Justice. The Court will then be able to impose the unspecified 'duties' incumbent on citizens of the 'Union' (Article 8.2), even though the British government claims that the pillar structures, which form the intergovernmental aspects of the 'Union', fall outside the Court's competence.

Edinburgh must reject the notion of the 'Union', and of the duties falling on its 'citizens'. The European Community is not a state, and it should never try to become one.

17

The European Court of Justice

We are told that the European Court can be relied on to enforce respect for the treaty in such a way that the Community does not become too centralised or intrusive. It is claimed that subsidiarity will help to create a climate in which the Court gives greater emphasis to the rights of member states.

Maastricht dramatically increases the power of the Community as a whole, and thereby increases the power of the Court. Above all, it allows the Court to move into governmental decision-making, the sphere for example of monetary union. This is a very dangerous development.

Moreover, to ask the Court to provide protection against further encroachments of Community law into national life is like asking the poacher to become the gamekeeper. Why, for example, has the Commission never been taken to the Court for failing to uphold the five declared principles of the Common Agricultural Policy? Why was it forced into unwelcome concessions on VAT harmonisation and the length of the working week?

It is widely recognised by expert legal opinion that the European Court of Justice has been one of the prime movers of European integration. It sees itself as having a central role in promoting European unity, and it has consistently favoured the most integrationist approach to disputes, frequently extending its own power in a series of seminal judgments. Even arch-federalists have been amazed by its integrationist zeal. In no sense can the Court be regarded as impartially holding the balance between the central European institutions and the member states.

On occasions, this extension of power has been explicitly based on what the Court thinks the treaties should say, rather than what they actually do say, a strange argument for a Court which is supposed to uphold a treaty. Professor T.J. Hartley has referred to this as 'revolting judicial behaviour'. In behaving in this way, the Court resembles the Commission, which has repeatedly abused its powers, even though the two institutions are supposed to be guardians of the treaty.

In the Maastricht treaty, the wordy aims of integration set out in the preamble, which the Court frequently uses as justification for its integrationist judgments, are even more far-reaching than before. The treaty itself is badly and ambiguously drafted, a disaster from a legal point of view. Most worrying is the new power which the Court will have over the governmental questions of monetary union and budget deficits. It is objectionable enough that the Commission and the bank, two undemocratic bodies, should be in charge of the economic policy of the Community: to give the Court competence to pronounce in disputes between the member states and these central institutions will snuff out the last flicker of democracy in the Community.

Edinburgh must reinforce the rule of law, but it cannot allow government by judges. The new sanctions available to the Court under Maastricht will not ensure this, unless the Court can be relied on to interpret the treaties fairly. A clause allowing a member state to secede from the Community should also be added, as a safeguard, for no such provision exists at present. Failure to do this will entangle member states in a powerful legal order from which it will be legally impossible for them to extricate themselves, even if the system is abused.

Why the line should be drawn at the Single European Act

We are told that our problems with the Commission come from abuses of the Single European Act.

But the SEA was about free trade and commerce, whereas **Maastricht** is about federal government. Even though the SEA was more precisely formulated than the Maastricht treaty, the Commission has successfully abused its power, accorded under Article 100A and similar provisions, and tried to interfere excessively; but the Maastricht treaty contains no provisions for containing such abuse, nor for nipping in the bud attempts to extend the Commission's power. The British government has recently given in, yet again, over VAT harmonisation, and reduced Britain's independence in the process to less than that of a state of the USA, where different sales taxes already apply in a federal country. If there had really been a commitment to decentralisation in Maastricht, then it is difficult to see how this measure could have been adopted. It is a serious failing of the Maastricht treaty that it added to the Community's powers, rather than reducing them.

Edinburgh should emphasise that the Single European Act can be made to work by eliminating abuses of procedure and of competence and by enforcing sanctions on countries that break the rules, as the government has proposed. However there is a vast amount of work to be done on the Single European Act to complete it and make it effective – rather than moving into areas of government under Maastricht which will create tensions, not trading opportunities. Edinburgh should emphasise the importance of keeping the Community together on a practicable basis.

19

Common foreign policy: bad in practice

We are told that unanimity has been preserved in the provisions for a common foreign policy.

Maastricht removes national independence in the implementation of foreign policy, where 'joint action' has been decided. Decisions on whether to take joint action are taken by unanimity, but once a joint action has been agreed in this way, member states are legally obliged to support it, and legally prevented from pursuing any national policy which would undermine the common position.

Article J.1.4 states:

The Member States shall support the Union's external and security policy unreservedly and in a spirit of loyalty and mutual solidarity. They shall refrain from any action which is contrary to the interests of the union or likely to impair its effectiveness as a cohesive force in international relations. The Council shall ensure that these principles are complied with.

How would this work in practice? 'Joint action' might, for instance, be 'to negotiate a peaceful settlement in Yugoslavia'. Clearly such an open-ended commitment is a blank cheque. It is apparent from the detailed formulation of the procedure to be followed, that joint action is intended for long-term aspects of foreign policy. Britain claims here, as elsewhere, that it has retarded over-ambitious plans for joint action. But once the decision has been taken to declare something joint action, a member state will have legally divested itself of all freedom to act independently in that area. At the time of unanimously voting on whether to take joint action, it may be impossible to predict what actions a member state will be legally obliged to undertake. Furthermore, the reliance on legalistic pieces of paper with lawyers and administrators scrambling about in an emergency trying to work out whether a policy comes within a joint action plan or not is positively dangerous to European and global security. The dividing line between foreign policy and defence can be very narrow. The loss of our pragmatic freedom of action is a serious failure.

Moreover, the institutions of the Community have not been as far separated out from this area of the treaty as the government claims. Although the Presidency will represent the Union in matters coming within the common foreign and security policy, and although it will be responsible for the implementation of common measures, Article J.5.3 states that 'the Commission shall be fully associated with these tasks'. It is disingenuous to claim as a victory that the Commission does not have the 'sole' right of initiative in this area.

To claim that foreign policy falls outside the competence of the European Court of Justice is also disingenuous. It is difficult to see how foreign policy could ever have come under the adjudication of the European Court of Justice, which normally pronounces on Community law, whereas foreign policy is not about legislation. None the less, the commitments quoted above, which oblige member states to accept joint action even when they have been outvoted will, like those of any other treaty, be legally enforceable by the International Court at the Hague.

Edinburgh should recognise that the countries of the European Community have a general desire to co-operate with one another, but that their interests and political integration have not reached such a level that they can be individually outvoted in foreign policy and legally forced to accept the decisions of the majority. Edinburgh must establish the principle of national independence in foreign policy, and free member states from the coercion of Maastricht.

20

Common foreign policy: wrong in principle

We are told that a common foreign policy will contribute to greater influence for the Community on the international stage.

Maastricht encourages the view that the European Community can act as if it were a single country, in economic and social policy as much as in foreign policy. But the attempt to link the foreign policies of the twelve into one in advance will lead to inertia. The idea that foreign policy can be managed with faxes and phone calls flying around the capitals of Europe in an attempt to reach a common position as a crisis unfolds is dangerously wrong. It shows a deeply bureaucratic misunderstanding of the way large-scale organisations should work.

In the Gulf War, it was not the UN which built the coalition, it was the United States and Britain in particular, with the self-assurance to move swiftly and to fight tyranny. Where foreign policy and defence policy is managed by a legalistic committee, the result is inertia. The determination to pursue a common foreign policy in Yugoslavia has produced nothing but disaster, deadlock and capitulation to German demands. Already, as the *Economist* noted on 1 August 1992, the WEU and NATO naval forces are both 'doing the same non-job' – 'the confusion will grow'. And any future aggressor will know that the Community will never do anything. In history, it has been the democratic nation-states which have stood up and fought for liberty, and the would-be supra-national empires which have tried to snuff it out.

Edinburgh should try to move away from this bureaucratic approach, which is as deadening in foreign policy as it is in other areas. In 1900, when Britain was the world's undisputed superpower, the staff of the Foreign Service based in London consisted of 40 people. Perhaps the past has something to teach us in this respect.

Political union

We are told that the European Community's underlying motivation has always been political and that 'those who suggest that in 1973 Britain only wanted to join the "Common Market" for free trade have got their history wrong'. This argument is wheeled out to justify the decisive increase in the Community's federal powers contained in the Maastricht treaty and sidesteps what everyone knows – which is that for decades the Community pursued a deceitful policy 'by stealth'.

Why otherwise does **Maastricht** change the name, 'European Economic Community' to 'European Community'? Why is the word 'Economic' dropped? Surely this illustrates the new political ambitions which the Community is giving itself for the first time.

When Britain joined in 1973, it was for economic reasons, re-affirmed in the 1975 referendum, and Edward Heath's White Paper explicitly ruled out political integration or federalism. It said:

> The Community is no federation of provinces or counties. It constitutes a community of great and established nations, each with its own personality and traditions. The practical working of the Community accordingly reflects the reality that sovereign governments are represented around the table. On a question where a government considers that vital national interests are involved, it is established that the decision should be unanimous. Like any other treaty, the Treaty of Rome commits its signatories to support agreed aims; but the commitment represents the voluntary undertaking of a sovereign state to observe policies which it has helped to form. There is no question of any erosion of national sovereignty. All the countries concerned recognise that an attempt to impose a majority view in a case where one or more

members consider their vital national interests to be at stake would imperil the very fabric of the Community.

How far, how very far, we have come since then.

Edinburgh would do well to insist that this excellent passage should be included as a preamble in the new treaty. It was the basis on which Britain joined, and it reflects the practices of the Community at the time. It would reaffirm that the Community has not abandoned its traditional and proper framework as a union of sovereign states.

22

Germany's new assertiveness

We are told that the Maastricht treaty will help bind Germany in, and that the new Anglo-German axis works to our advantage.

Maastricht was largely dreamed up by the German government. The Konrad Adenauer Stiftung (the official think-tank of the ruling Christian Democratic Party) boasts that the Franco-German initiative in April 1990, which ultimately led to the Maastricht treaty, was 'primarily formulated in the Federal Chancellery in Bonn'. Horst Teltschik, Helmut Kohl's former long-serving foreign policy adviser, has said, 'We asked the French to take the initiative' over European integration. By common admission, it was the Germans who pressed for the greatest degree of federalist integration during the Maastricht negotiations, and, in general, all their demands were met. It is curious to argue that Chancellor Kohl helped Britain to derogate from the most uncomfortable parts of the Maastricht treaty, such as EMU and the Social Chapter, when it was the Germans who had pressed so hard for these in the first place, and when the underlying federal push remains in the treaty anyway.

Germany has for long suffered from being an economic giant but a political pygmy. She seeks to establish security on her borders by expanding her influence and control. She wants to assume a higher political profile under the guise of 'Europe'. She has for long demanded that the European Central Bank be sited in Germany, presumably so that it is independent of everybody but herself. Her massive trade surplus comes overwhelmingly from the Community, and she seeks to protect these markets in order to expand and to survive. (Britain's own trade deficit with Germany is especially crippling, and it is still increasing: it now represents three-quarters of our deficit with the Community as a whole, and is higher than it has been for a year.) Germany knows that countries which are in thrall to her economically will not be able to oppose her politically, in the Council of Ministers, for instance. The new Europe will be a German Europe.

Ever since the ten-point plan for reunification, announced in December 1989, in the absence of any consultation with her allies, Germany has been becoming more and more assertive. Her pressure for representation on the UN Security Council, for more seats in the European Parliament, for her own policy over Yugoslavia, over the European fighter, the German-USSR treaty, the demand that we renounce our £2 billion rebate from the Community, the recent raising of interest rates, despite public and humiliating pleading from her European partners – all these underline her new, higher profile. But a European Community modelled on the Federal Republic's constitution will only entrench German hegemony over the whole continent.

Edinburgh must address this ominous geopolitical development. A balance of interest and power in Europe, both East and West, is not compatible with a tight core of countries, dominated by Germany, dictating policy to the periphery. The nineteenth-century federal German Empire grew out of the German Customs Union over a period of forty years: it is essential to take the long-term view. We want to work within the Community with all member states, including Germany, but not on her terms. Otherwise it is not a Community.

23

Defence

We are told that we are not going to have a European defence policy, and that we do not want to undermine NATO.

Maastricht uses the vague expression 'the eventual framing of a common defence policy, which might in time lead to a common defence'. It also refers to the Western European Union as 'an integral part of the development of the Union', and the Union 'requests the WEU to elaborate and implement decisions and actions of the Union which have defence implications'. Almost immediately after Maastricht, France and Germany had formed their own Franco-German ('European') army unilaterally: no doubt the delay of a few weeks is what was meant by 'in time'. These countries freely refer to the WEU as the defence arm of the Community. The Union has the right, under Article F, to provide itself with the means necessary to attain its objectives and carry through its policies, and already signs of this are apparent in the status of the British warship due for the Adriatic under the aegis of WEU, in line with federalist policy. As the *Economist* noted in August 1992, 'On this evidence the WEU is an alliance divider'. We have gone along with this in what is becoming an increasingly familiar way.

Edinburgh should reaffirm the importance of the Atlantic Alliance as an integral part of the unity and security of Europe as a whole, rather than merely making concession to the membership of NATO of some member states. It should insist on a change in policy by those countries, such as Germany, France, Italy and Spain, who have concluded treaties with the former Soviet Union which, in the opinion of defence analysts, crucially undermine NATO.

The right of community nationals to vote in elections

We are told that, under Maastricht, European Community nationals resident in another Community country will have the right, as 'citizens of the Union' to vote and stand as candidates in local and European elections of the country in which they live.

Maastricht refers to the right to vote in 'municipal elections' (Article 8b). But the word 'municipal', under international law, has nothing to do with local government: it means 'national', as opposed to 'international'. When the European Court of Justice found against Italy in 1972, it declared that 'the treaty entails a definitive limitation of the sovereign rights of member states against which no provisions of municipal law (i.e. national law), whatever their nature, can be legally invoked'. This judgment is central to the establishment of the superiority of Community law over national law, and the use of the word 'municipal' in this context appears to leave the field wide open for the same interpretation to be given to the word when it refers to 'municipal elections'.

If the Court did decide on this interpretation of Maastricht (overriding British legislation), it would mean that a Greek or an Italian would have the automatic right to vote in British elections, and even perhaps to become an MP at Westminster.

If the intention was only to allow EC nationals to vote in local or regional elections, then why were the words 'local and regional' not used? It is another serious omission from the treaty that these crucial matters were not clearly defined.

Edinburgh should revoke the very notion of 'citizenship of the Union', for it is central to the whole federalist concept. It should define its terms with crystal clarity. The right to vote is a central aspect of national sovereignty, and if foreigners are to enjoy it (certain categories of foreigners already do so under British law), then decisions to this effect should be taken bilaterally, not imposed centrally, as Maastricht does.

25

The Cohesion Fund

We were told that we would resist a cohesion fund, under which Britain would be forced to pay subsidy to the poorer countries of the Community.

Article 130d of the **Maastricht** treaty (Title XIV: 'Economic and Social Cohesion') says,

> The Council shall before 31st December 1993, set up a Cohesion Fund to provide a financial contribution to projects in the fields of environment and trans-European networks in the area of transport infrastructure.

The Protocol on Economic and Social Cohesion commits us to

> financial contributions in these fields in Member States with a per capita GNP of less than 90% of the Community average, which have a programme leading to the fulfilment of the conditions of economic convergence set out in Article 104c [which concerns budget deficits].

This means that we are obliged to pay for the adjustment of other member states to the convergence criteria for Economic and Monetary Union, whether we are in it or not, such as by paying to reduce their budget deficits in order to help them meet the convergence criteria, which they are increasingly finding it impossible to do.

Jacques Delors has already called for an increase in Community spending over the next five years of £12 billion – an annual growth rate of 5% – justifying this increase on the grounds of 'our duties as countries of the North to those of the South'. It is difficult to see how the British government can both press for the ratification of the treaty and at the same time refuse to pay the extra expenditure to which they are committed by it. Moreover, as Andrew Scott of Heriot-Watt University indicated in *Forum on Europe* (July 1992), the Delors II package 'represents a rate of growth of public spending that is unlikely to be matched by national budgets over the same period'. The money is simply not there – as the USA is also discovering in its own federal dilemma. Forcing a transfer of resources merely creates problems.

Edinburgh must remove these blank cheques from the treaty. If a government does not have control over its own finances, and if it is obliged by the treaty to spend them according to the Community's wishes, then it has no more status that a charge-capped local council. We must avoid the mistakes already evident in, for example, Australia and the USA. Meanwhile the structural funds are to go up by 6% in the next five years, not to mention the CAP increases and the endemic and massive fraud which this generates.

The British opt-out of the Social Chapter

We are told that Britain has opted out on Community Social Policy, and that 'Britain will not be subject to the damaging regulations which are likely to flow from the new Social Chapter' (Douglas Hurd, 14 May 1992). We have been told that these would cost us £5 billion a year and the loss of our attraction to investors such as the Japanese.

Maastricht seems to do little to prevent the imposition of Community Social Policy in Britain. The Community will be able to use Article 118A of the Single European Act (as well as Article 100A, which provides for majority voting) to introduce Social Chapter provisions under the guise of health and safety at work and single market measures. The 48-hour working week, originally a Social Chapter provision, was reintroduced and successfully forced onto an unwilling Britain. It is highly unlikely that the European Court of Justice would allow a member state to plead that such things did not fall within the Community's competence. If loopholes in the Single European Act have been exploited, why were these not closed under Maastricht?

Edinburgh should push for treaty amendments to make these abuses impossible. This should have been done at Maastricht. The opt-out from the Social Chapter is highly questionable.

The illusion that the ERM and EMU are good for jobs

We are told that our future is irrevocably in the Community, and especially in its monetary arrangements, because our economy needs the trade which flows from it in order to sustain jobs.

Maastricht commits us to membership of the ERM, and to accepting monetary union in the Community. Since Britain has been a member of the ERM, unemployment has risen by one million. As the *Daily Telegraph* has written, 'We joined at the wrong exchange rate, at the wrong time, and for the wrong reasons.' The *Financial Times* has pointed out that inflation is no lower than it was in the 1980s, when we got it out of the system.

We are now obliged to maintain high interest rates because the German government is fuelling inflation by providing subsidised credit and soft loans for the reconstruction of East Germany (from which they will ultimately profit), and refusing to finance this by tax.

Germany never takes the needs of other countries into consideration when deciding interest rates. While the other member states rely on exchange rates to control inflation, Germany ignores them and concentrates on her interest rates instead, as was illustrated by the last increase, on 16 July.

The other member states now are paying in the form of high interest rates, high mortgages and a deep recession for the rebuilding of Eastern Germany, and for keeping West German tax levels down. It is impossible to say for how long this situation may continue. The United States and Japan, which are not members of fixed exchange rate mechanisms, have significantly lower interest rates than we do.

Edinburgh must detach Britain from this straitjacket. A recent study by the University of California at Berkeley concluded that it is the peripheral countries (the UK and Southern Europe) which are most likely to suffer regional shocks from EMU, far more seriously than the core countries. Accepting EMU will entrench the German domination of Europe, committing Britain to remain eternally peripheral to Europe's central monetary and economic considerations, destroying jobs, the economy, and any hope of recovery. Far from containing inflation, hitching ourselves to the German economy could in future increase it, and the Central Bankers cannot guarantee to prevent this. German interest rates and our own are only nearer to each other because the Germans, for their own internal reasons, raised theirs. We are simply giving away control over our own economy. A Bank of England on the New Zealand model would provide democratic independence on our own terms – and low inflation.

28

Our honour is at stake

We are told that to abandon the treaty would weaken our influence and cast doubt upon our integrity (Douglas Hurd), or that having given our word, we should keep it (the Prime Minister). We are told that we are bound by the Conservative Manifesto to ratify the treaty. We are also told that a referendum is not in the parliamentary tradition.

All countries have to ratify **Maastricht** for it to enter into force. The ratification process is an integral part of signing a treaty, and we are entirely within our rights to reject it once its real content becomes clear to Parliament. The Danes were similarly within their rights to do the same thing. The government claims that it has obtained the right for parliament to decide on whether to join monetary union at a future date but at the same time insists that parliament agrees not to veto EMU for Europe as a whole – which includes the United Kingdom.

There was no specific commitment in the Conservative Manifesto to the Maastricht treaty. The votes in the House of Commons in the debate in December 1991 and on the Second Reading of the Maastricht Bill were subject to a three-line whip, and they were usually held in the absence of treaty texts. Unlike in 1970, there was no White Paper.

At the general election, all three parties were favourable to closer integration. The voters had no real choice, and Dicey argues that, in such a case, a referendum is justified. In any event, when the very future of the free choice of the voter to choose his or her economic and monetary policy options in a general election is at risk under EMU, the case for a referendum becomes unassailable.

What has happened to the honourable Tory doctrine, 'Trust the people'? The Maastricht treaty will profoundly affect the way this country is governed. It is the most important constitutional change in Britain for three hundred years. A referendum on this momentous issue is the only honourable choice, particularly in the absence of a free vote in the House of Commons or even a White Paper.

When the *Woman's Own* opinion poll in August 1992 shows that nine out of ten do not know what the ERM is and that one in two think the ecu is an animal, the case for a clear, agreed and impartial layman's guide to Maastricht, distributed throughout the United Kingdom, becomes overwhelming.

Accusations that those who want to renegotiate Maastricht are 'political spivs' overlook the main feature of the spiv – a neurotic failure properly to explain the small print to an unsuspecting public.

29

Where do we propose to go instead?

We are told there is no alternative, and we are asked a number of rhetorical questions to prove it.

Where do we start from? The Treaty of Rome and the Single European Act constitute the European Economic Community, which encourages free trade and political co-operation in some areas. They will remain in place if Maastricht is not ratified. We are happy to be members of this European Community, but we are not prepared to sacrifice democracy on its altar with all the dangerous instability that would create.

Where are we going? Under Maastricht, the bureaucratic nature of the EEC has not been reformed, as it should have been: it has been intolerably strengthened, suffocating democratic and parliamentary control throughout the Community. It is imperative to turn the Community away from this unhealthy and damaging development to an open democratic way forward – a fresh start.

Who is with us? The Danish vote was the first sign of growing discontent with the direction the Community is taking. Repeated opinion polls in Britain show opposition to further European integration to be above 60%. 80% of Germans do not want to give up their currency. Opposition is substantial in France. The more people are told what is in the treaty the less they like it. They have not been adequately informed in layman's language, which is a disgrace. Meetings, initially prompted by British MPs, have been taking place throughout Europe with other anti-federalist national parliamentarians including those from Eastern Europe and EFTA. They are very much with us. Although we do not have equivalent resources to the Europropaganda machine we remain undeterred.

Europe: The Crunch

With whom are we going to negotiate? There is a happy coincidence of events which places Britain in the Presidency when this latest Franco-German project has failed, and when those countries are pre-occupied with internal problems. The Danish vote has given us a unique opportunity to re-endorse democracy in Europe. All twelve countries simply must renegotiate and comply with the rule of law. To do otherwise is to encourage bureaucracy and authoritarianism.

Who is going to talk to us? In 1938 people said that no one would listen if Britain protested. We won then because we took a stand on the principle of freedom and democracy. These are now at stake all over Europe, threatened by suffocating bureaucracy. We are prepared to negotiate with anybody, but not if the language is simply one of threats, as it has been in the past. Some have been threatening to exclude Denmark. That is an unacceptable basis for negotiation, but this is where we came in eighteen months ago.

Is anyone listening?